AUSTRALIA

Connie Bickman

Published by Abdo & Daughters, 4940 Viking Drive, Suite 622, Edina, Minnesota 55435.

Library bound edition distributed by Rockbottom Books, Pentagon Tower, P.O. Box 36036, Minneapolis, Minnesota 55435.

Printed in the United States.

Cover Photo credit: Connie Bickman, GeoIMAGERY
Interior Photo credits: Connie Bickman, GeoIMAGERY, Natural Selection page 7
Map created by John Hamilton

Edited by Julie Berg

LIBRARY OF CONGRESS CATALOGING-IN-PUBLICATION DATA

Bickman, Connie.
     Australia / Connie Bickman.
         p.   cm. -- (Through the Eyes of Children)
     Includes index.
     ISBN 1-56239-326-X
     1. Australia--Juvenile literature.   [1. Australia--Social life and customs.]
     I. Title.II. Series.
     DU96.B53   1994
     994--dc20   94-13308
                                                  CIP
                                                      AC

Contents

Introduction to Australia

AUSTRALIA

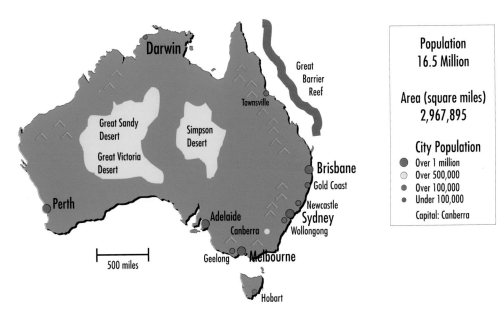

Population
16.5 Million

Area (square miles)
2,967,895

City Population
- Over 1 million
- Over 500,000
- Over 100,000
- Under 100,000

Capital: Canberra

Australia was once part of a giant land called Gondwana.
It broke away and became its own continent.

It is a land where kangaroo and furry koala bear live.
It is a land of crocodile and funny lizards that wear collars
around their necks.

Most people speak English in Australia.
But they have different names for many things.
In Australia the country is called the outback.
Some of the land is called the bush.
Swamps are called billabongs.

Australia has beautiful rainforests.
It has mountains and tall waterfalls.
It has islands with sandy beaches.
Australia has hot dry deserts.
It has the Great Barrier Reef full of tropical fish.

Australia has the biggest rock in the world.
It is called Ayres (AY-ers) Rock .
Ayres Rock is in the middle of the country.
It covers over 1,000 acres.

Australia is full of wonderful stories.
These stories are called legends.
They tell of *Dreamtime* and *Rainbow Serpents.*
They tell of the beginning of the land.
They tell of the Aboriginie people.
They were the first people to live in Australia.

Australia has many interesting people.
They are people just like you.
Some live in big or small cities.
Some live in the outback or on the coast.

The people of Australia are friendly.
They sound like Crocodile Dundee when they talk.

Would you like to visit Australia?
Let's meet some of the children who live there.

Meet The Children of Australia

These two boys are good friends.
They are both Australian.
One of the boys is an Aboriginie.
Aboriginies are the natives of Australia.
That means they were the first people to live in Australia.
These two boys live and play the same.
The only thing different about them is their color.

These boys are brothers.
They are also friends.
They help take care of each other.
They help their mom and dad.

What's Good to Eat?

This girl is selling sandwiches in the city.
Do you think she has peanut butter and jelly?
In most parts of Australia the children eat what you do.
Did you know they even have McDonalds?
But they also eat crocodile sandwiches!

What Do They Wear?

T-shirts and jeans are favorite clothes.
For special dances they sometimes wear grass skirts.
This boy is from North Queensland.
He is wearing a skirt made of long grasses.
Do you see the handprint on his back?
This is a symbol of his people.
It tells what tribe he belongs to.
It is painted from a clay called ochre.
He is an Aboriginie.
He lives in the outback.
It is hot there.

This boy is wearing a hat with neck and ear flaps—and it's summer!
Do you know why?
He doesn't want to get a sunburn.
The hottest months in Australia are December through March.
That would be during their summer.
The coldest months are May to August.
That is during Australia's winter.

This boy is wearing a T-shirt and shorts.
He also has a baseball hat.
The hat on the ground is worn by many Australians.
He is also holding a flashlight.
In Australia, a flashlight is called a torch.

Where Do They Live?

Houses in the cities are very
nice, and look like yours.
Houses in the outback are
sometimes made of tin.

This is the famous Opera House in Sydney.
It is a beautiful building.
It is in the harbor where people in boats can see it.
Do you think it looks like a butterfly?

Getting Around

Most families drive trucks or jeeps in the outback.
The roads are rough and very bumpy.

The dirt on the road is red.
Shoes and clothes get red from
the dust.

This is a very old ship. Does it
look like it belongs in a city? It
gives rides to people who want to
see the buildings from the water.

What Are Traditions?

Traditions are the things people do over and over again.
Celebrating Christmas with your family is a tradition.
The Aboriginies have beliefs and legends in their traditions.
This Aboriginal boy is dressed for a celebration.
The celebration is called a corroboree.
When he is not at the corroboree,
he wears T-shirts and jeans just like you do.
He also drinks and eats many of the same things you do.

Do you know how these handprints were made?
An Aboriginal elder placed his hand on the rock.
Then he spit red ochre onto the rock like a stencil.
Only important men were allowed to do this.
It was a symbol that marked their territory.

Just For Fun!

The children of Australia like to have fun, too.
They like to run and play.
They are just like you!
This boy is playing a didgeridoo.
It is a popular musical instrument in Australia.
It is a made from a small tree.
Termites ate the middle of the tree, making it hollow.
Then it was painted and made into a didgeridoo.
To make music you blow into one end.

You do not stop to breathe.
Instead, you breathe in and out while you play.
The didgeridoo has its own songs.
Its music cannot be played on other instruments.

These young boys are dancing.
The name of their dance is "Crocodile".
Can you tell who is the crocodile
and who is the hunter?
The boys learned the dance from their fathers and
grandfathers.
It is a very old dance.
Children in Australia also play kickball, soccer and
other sports.

How Do They Work?

Children in Australia have to work, too.
This little boy is working.
He is taking care of a camel.
His father owns the Blue Gum Camel Farm.
Riding a camel is fun.
It is also bumpy.
Be careful—
camels like to spit!
Did you know that camels live to be 40 years old?

This boy is fishing.
He has made a spear from a stick.
He is trying to spear a fish in the river.
Do you think he will have fish for dinner?

Australia has a lot of cowboys.
They ride horses.
They work on cattle and sheep ranches.
This cowboy is on a cattle drive.
He is helping take the cows to market.
Do you see the windmill?
It is used to make electricity.
Do you see the big tank?
It is a water tank.

School is Fun!

These girls are on a field trip with their school.
They are learning about history.
Some of the history of Australia is written on rocks and in caves.
It is written with pictures of animals and people.
These stories are called petroglyphs.
Many of the petroglyphs tell of *Dreamtime*.
Dreamtime is the story of the creation of the land of Australia.
Don't you think a huge rock makes a funny history book?

Their Land

The land of Australia can be very unusual.
It has beautiful oceans and lots of fish.
It has big hot deserts.
It has funny rocks and huge mountains.

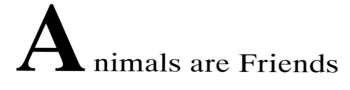nimals are Friends

Do you think it would be fun to play with a kangaroo?
There are many kinds of kangaroo in Australia.
They all have strong back legs and powerful tails.
They move by jumping and leaping.
They have pockets in their stomachs where they
carry their babies.
Smaller cousins of the kangaroo are called wallaby.

This bird is called an emu.
An emu is a cousin to the ostrich.
It is as tall as a man.
It is very strong and runs very fast.
The female emu lays big green eggs.
The male emu sits on the nest until the eggs hatch.

Children are the same everywhere

It is fun to see how children in other countries live. Many children have similar ways of doing things. Did you see things that were the same as in your life? They may play and go to school and have families just like you. They may work, travel and dress different than you.

One thing is always the same. That is a smile. If you smile at other children, they will smile back. That is how you make new friends. It's fun to have new friends all over the world!

Glossary

Aboriginal - pertaining to an Aboriginie.

Aboriginal elder - an old man. As people get older they are considered by their people to be wiser.

Aboriginie - first people of a country; natives.

Billabong - swamp or low lying water area.

Bush - remote desert-like areas of Australia.

Corroboree - native dance festival or celebration for Australian Aboriginies.

Didgeridoo - musical instrument made from a tree.

Dreamtime - Aboriginal stories and legends that tell of the creation and beginning of the land of Australia.

Emu - a large bird that is a cousin to the ostrich.

Gondwana - a supercontinent that broke apart, creating many smaller continents, including Australia.

Ochre - natural yellow or red clay that is ground into powder to make paint.

Outback - countryside where there are few towns and people.

Petroglyphs - rock carvings and paintings.

Pinnacles - strange limerock formations in Western Australia.

Rainbow Serpent - the Aboriginies believe that the rivers and mountains were created by this large snake as it crawled along the ground.

Symbol - sign telling about something or someone.

Termites - very small insects that eat wood or earth.

Territory - land or area.

Wallaby - smaller cousin to the kangaroo.

Index

About the Author/Photographer

Connie Bickman is a photojournalist whose photography has won regional and international awards.

She is retired from a ten-year newspaper career and currently owns her own portrait studio and art gallery. She is an active freelance photographer and writer whose passion it is to travel the far corners of the world in search of adventure and the opportunity to photograph native cultures.

She is a member of the National Press Association and the Minnesota Newspaper Photographers Association.